The Sweet Life

A JOURNAL

Laura Stoddart

CHRONICLE BOOKS

SAN FRANCISCO

First published in United States in 2005 by Chronicle Books LLC
First published in Great Britain 2003 by Orion Books,
a division of the Orion Publishing Group Ltd.

Images and quotations from
The Sweet Life: Reflections on Home and Garden
by Laura Stoddart
Published by Chronicle Books 2001

ISBN: 0-8118-4936-8

Distributed in Canada by
Raincoast Books
9050 Shaughnessy Street
Vancouver, B.C. V6P 6E5

CHRONICLE BOOKS
85 Second Street
San Francisco, CA 94105
www.chroniclebooks.com

God Almightie first planted a Garden. And indeed, it is the Purest of Humane pleasure. It is the Greatest Refreshment to the Spirits of Man.

Francis Bacon (1561–1626) *Essays*

A garden must be looked unto
and dressed as the body.

George Herbert (1593–1633)

Is the fancy too far brought, that this love for gardens is a reminiscence haunting the race of that remote time when but two persons existed – a gardener named Adam and a gardener's wife called Eve?

Alexander Smith (1830–1867)

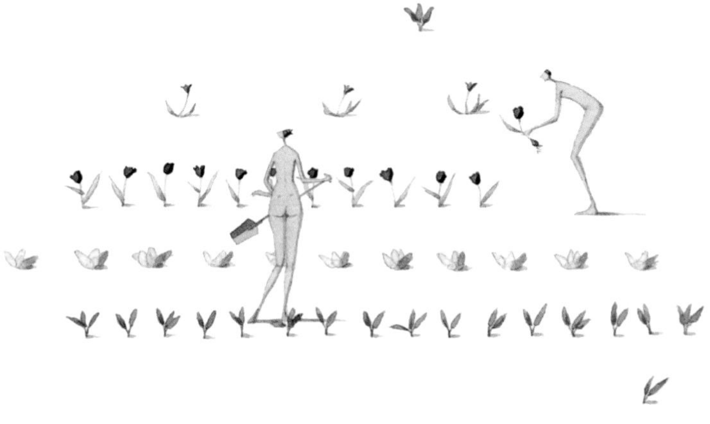

A modest garden contains, for those who know how to look and to wait, more instruction than a library.

Henri Frédéric Amiel (1821–1881)

Woman has no seductions for the man who cannot
keep his eyes off his magnolias.

Anonymous

The best way to get real enjoyment out of the garden is to put on a wide straw hat, hold a little trowel in one hand and a cool drink in the other, and tell the man where to dig.

Charles Barr

Trees are the best monuments that a man can erect to his own memory. They speak his praises without flattery, and they are blessings to children yet unborn.

Lord Orrery (1707–1762)

My garden sweet, enclosed with walles strong,
Enbanked with benches to sytt and take my rest:
The knotts so enknotted, it cannot be exprest,
With arbors and alyes so pleasaunt and so dulce.

George Cavendish (1499–1561)

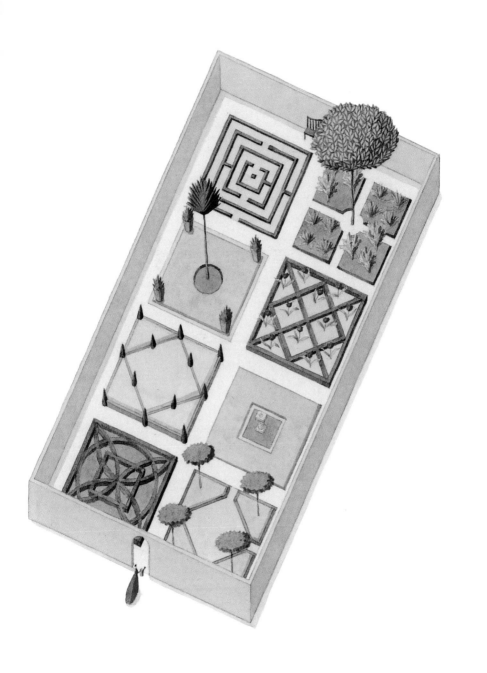

Even the clipt yews interest me; and if I found one in any garden that should be mine, in the shape of a peacock, I should be as proud to keep his tail well spread as the man who first carved him.

Robert Southey (1774–1843)

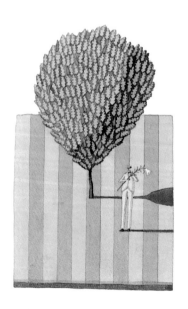

A lawn, a lily
  And a lilac tree:
They take a lot of beating,
  Wherever they be.

Reginald Arkell (1882–1959) *New Saying*

In nature everything is distinct, yet nothing defined into absolute independent singleness.

William Wordsworth (1770–1850) from *Guide to the Lakes*

Who loves a garden, loves a greenhouse too.

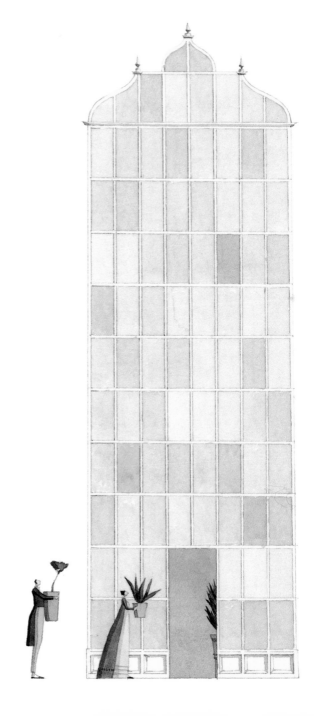

To me the meanest flower that blows can give
Thoughts that do often lie too deep for tears.

William Wordsworth (1770–1850)
Ode: Imitations of Immortality

You buy some flowers for your table;
You tend them tenderly as you're able;
You fetch them water from hither and thither –
What do you get for it all? They wither.

Samuel Hoffenstein (1890–1947)

A low hedge is easily leapt over.

Proverb

Snow, snow, snow
I want to wash my feet, my hair,
   my hands, and teeth, in snow.

Anonymous

"to sit in the shade on a fine day, and look upon verdure, is the most perfect refreshment."

Jane Austen (1775–1817) from *Mansfield Park*

Then in we went, to the garden glorious
Like to a place, of pleasure most solacious
With flora paynted and wrought curiously
In divers knottes of marveylous greatnes.

Anonymous

A garden is a delight to the eye, and a solace to the soil; it soothes angry passions, and produces that pleasure which is a foretaste of Paradise.

Sa' Di (1184–1291)

GWENDOLEN I had no idea there were any flowers in the country.

CECILY Oh, flowers are as common here, Miss Fairfax, as people are in London.

Oscar Wilde (1854–1900) *The Importance of Being Earnest*

(Gardening) is not graceful, and it makes one hot; but it is a blessed sort of work, and if Eve had had a spade in Paradise and known what to do with it, we should not have had all that sad business of the apple.

Elizabeth, Countess von Arnim (1866–1941)

Why are there trees I never walk under but large and melodious thoughts descend upon me?

Walt Whitman (1819–1892)

What a man needs in gardening is a cast-iron back with a hinge in it.

Charles Dudley Warner (1829–1900)

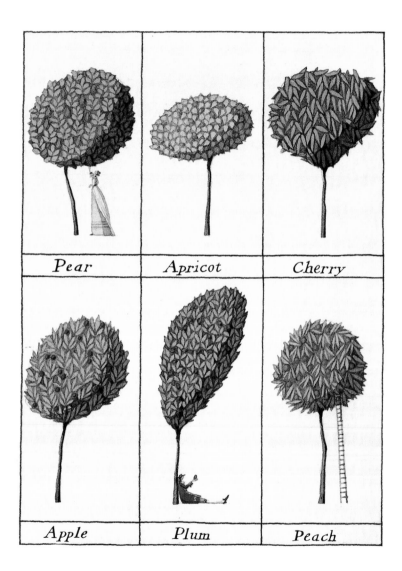

| Pear | Apricot | Cherry |
| Apple | Plum | Peach |

I like to think how Shakespeare pruned his rose,
And ate his pippin in his orchard close.

William Rose Benét (1886–1950)

A gardener's work is never at an end.

John Evelyn (1620–1706) from *Kalendarium Hortense*

Did you ever meet a gardener, who, however fair his ground, was absolutely content and pleased? . . . Is there not ever some grand mistake to be remedied next summer?

The Rev. Samuel Hole (1819–1904)

What is a weed? A plant whose virtues have not yet
been discovered.

Ralph Waldo Emerson (1803–1882) from *Fortune of the Republic*

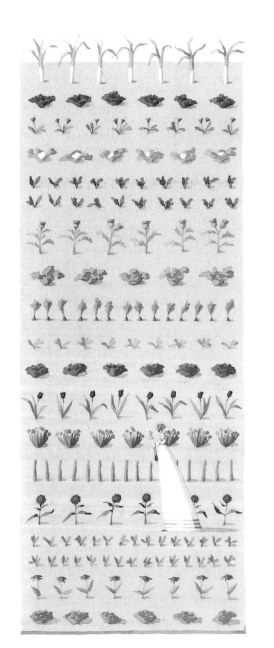

A garden without trees scarcely deserves to be called a garden.

Canon Henry Ellacombe (1790–1885)

Poems are made by fools like me,
But only God can make a tree.

Joyce Kilmer (1886–1918) from *Trees*

Oh, Adam was a gardener, and God who made him sees
That half a proper gardener's work is done upon his knees.

Rudyard Kipling (1865–1936) from *The Glory of the Garden*

Who has seen the wind?
  Neither you nor I;
But when the trees bow down their heads
  The wind is passing by.

Christina Rossetti (1830–1894) from *The Wind*

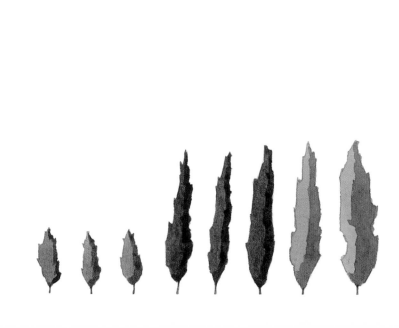

Merry and tranquil! Tedious and brief!
That is, hot ice and wondrous strange snow.

William Shakespeare (1564–1616) *A Midsummer Night's Dream*

A hedge between keeps friendship green.

Proverb

The day, water, sun, moon, night – I do not have to purchase these things with money.

Plautus (c.254–184 B.C.)

If I keep a green bough in my heart,
the singing bird will come.

Anonymous